The Blessed Hope

The Blessed Hope

KENNETH G. SYMES

ARPress
ILLUMINATING IDEAS.
EMPOWERING VOICES

ARPress
45 Dan Road Suite 5
Canton MA 02021
Hotline: 1(888) 821-0229
Fax: 1(508) 545-7580

Ordering Information:
Quantity sales. Special discounts are available on quantity purchases by corporations, associations, and others. For details, contact the publisher at the address above.

Printed in the United States of America.

ISBN-13:   Softcover   979-8-89330-665-1
           eBook   979-8-89330-664-4

Library of Congress Control Number: 2024902465

All Bible quotations are taken

from The King James Version.

TABLE OF CONTENTS

PREFACE

We are living in the shadows of the seven year Tribulation period, biblically known as the seventieth week of Daniel. This seismic prophetic event recorded by both the Hebrew Prophets in the Tenach (Old Testament) and the Jewish Apostles in the New Covenant (New Testament) revealed the almost unbelievable details of what might be referred to as one's worst nightmare...except worse. The Messiah Jesus declared, in what is referred to as the "Olivet Discourse", it will be the worst time in all of history, either in the past or in the future. It is incredible to think that such devastating events as spelled out in the book of the Revelation could actually occur and be compressed into such a short time period as the seven year Tribulation. But nevertheless, according to God, it is coming and I believe sooner than most think.

The good news is that the Bible-believing followers of Jesus, the Christ, have a reason to rejoice, in spite of all the gloom that is coming down the pike. It is called the "Blessed Hope",...the confident unshakeable belief that the generation of believers that would be alive when the Tribulation Period plays out, will be spared God's discipline upon His people Israel (whom He loves), the wrath of God poured out upon this sin-cursed world including those who dare to rebel and oppose Him, and to put down Satan and his thugs.

Not only are we rapidly moving headlong towards the Tribulation Period, but it seems as though Satan is very busy seeking to discredit, confuse and tear down the True Church and its precious doctrinal beliefs. This book on the blessed hope by Kenneth Symes comes at a very appropriate time in history. I am thankful that he has dealt with this doctrine in a clear and precise manner.

Stanley Rosenthal

National Field Director

Jewish Awareness Ministries, Inc

ACKNOWLEDGEMENTS

This book has been written because of the encouragement of several of my friends for which I am grateful. Special thanks must go to Dr. John Williamson, my pastor, who not only encouraged me to write this book, but who took the time to critique and edit my manuscript. He also listened and responded to me as I bounced thoughts off him as I was thinking through some of the issues. I also thank Terry Moffitt and Stan Rosenthal who critiqued and helped to edit this manuscript. Hopefully, they were the iron that sharpened iron in the writing of this small book. Thank you so very much for your help and encouragement to bring this book about.

THE BLESSED HOPE

By: Kenneth G. Symes

INTRODUCTION

The blessed hope! What is it? Why is it important for us to understand it? The answer to the second question may be answered simply in the words of the Apostle John as recorded in I John 3:3. *"And every man that hath this hope in him purifieth himself, even as he is pure."* There is no greater incentive to godly living than the hope of our Lord's soon return. John also tells us what the Blessed Hope is: *"Beloved, now are we the sons of God, and it doeth not yet appear what we shall be: but we know that, when he shall appear, we shall be like him; for we shall see him as he is."* (I John 3:2).

The purpose of the Christian life is to allow the Holy Spirit to change us into the image of our precious Lord. Paul puts it this way: *"But we all, with open face beholding as in a glass the glory of the Lord, are changed into the same image from glory to glory even as by the Spirit of the Lord"* (II cor. 3:18). In I Corinthians 15:51 Paul stated: *"Behold, I show you a mystery; We shall not all sleep, but we shall all be changed."* There is a central theme here. That theme is change. The promise is that we shall be changed into the image of Christ; that is, ultimately made perfect (complete). This process begins the moment we are saved and continues until we enter into His presence either through the grave or at His appearing. Paul said that we are being changed from glory to glory into His image. That is a present process. Both Paul and John state that the process is complete when we see Him at His appearing. Jesus Himself indicated the process for this transformation when He said: *"But seek ye first the kingdom of God and his righteousness..."* (Matt. 6:33a). All agree that this process moves forward, while we are here, as we focus on Jesus and His righteousness. The Holy Spirit places within us the desire to be like Him and He empowers the transformation.

What true believer does not look forward to the day when he stands in his Lord's presence and hears Him say: "Well done, thou good and faithful servant?" Thus, the matter of our Lord's appearing is a critical issue not only for the future but for our immediate needs as well.

There are many opinions relating to His appearing. As one who spends much time witnessing, I am often confronted with the statement: "Well, that is your opinion or interpretation." But Biblical issues should never be a matter of opinion! Is it not our responsibility, as His children, to study God's Word carefully, not to prove that our ideas are right but to find God's mind on whatever matter we are researching? Is that not what Peter was stressing when he wrote: *"Knowing this first that no prophecy of the scripture is of any private interpretation."* (II Peter 1:20)? If one believes the Bible to be God's inerrant, infallible Word and that there are no contradictions, why should the finding of God's mind on any matter be so difficult? Absolutely establishing God's mind on a matter negates opinion or interpretation allowing us to proclaim God's Word with the full authority of "Thus saith the LORD!" Surely, that is the kind of preaching we so desperately need from our pulpits today!

Absolutely establishing God's mind on a matter also enables us to understand the vital relationship that exists between all doctrines. As you read this book consider the vital relationship between one's understanding of the Rapture and the doctrines of Israel, the Church, the Atonement, the Holy Spirit, and the character of God. You will see that how one views the blessed hope will greatly affect the rest of his theology. This alone makes a study of the blessed hope an essential study.

The Church and Israel

One major issue that often confuses the believer in understanding the blessed hope is the relationship between Israel and the Church. If we are to fully understand the blessed hope, we must first understand that the Church and Israel in God's Word are two different and separate entities. There are two authors who deal with this subject admirably. Dr. C. I. Scofield in his book entitled: "Rightly Dividing The Word Of Truth", notes several contrasts between Israel and the Church. He states: "Comparing what is said in Scripture concerning Israel and the Church, he (the student) finds that in origin, calling, promise, worship, principles of conduct, and future destiny – all is contrast."[i] The calling of Israel is earthly (Gen. 12:1; Deut. 8:7-9), whereas the calling of the Church is heavenly (Heb. 3:1; Phil. 3:20; I Peter. 1:4). So the incentive to godliness for Israel is earthly; whereas the incentive for the Church is heavenly. Israel was to be governed by law (Deut. 28), whereas the Church is governed by Grace. Israel was instructed to worship only in one place approaching God only through a priest; whereas the church is free to worship wherever two or three are gathered (Matt. 18:20) and may enter boldly into His presence without the assistance of a priest (Heb. 4:16). The prophesied future destiny for Israel is the establishment of an earthly Kingdom from which Messiah Himself shall rule not only Israel but the whole earth. However, the Church will be removed from the earth to take up its abode in Heaven (John 14:1-3).

Dr. Lewis Sperry Chafer in his book "Systematic Theology", Volume IV, sets forth 24 contrasts between Israel and the Church. Dr. J. D. Pentecost outlines these contrasts as follows: "(1) the extent of Biblical revelation: Israel –nearly four-fifths of the Bible; Church –about one fifth. (2) The Divine purpose: Israel –the earthly promises in the covenants; Church –the heavenly promises in the gospel. (3) The seed of Abraham: Israel –the physical seed, of whom some become a spiritual seed; Church –a spiritual seed. (4) Birth: Israel –physical birth that brings relationship; Church –spiritual birth that brings relationship. (5) Headship: Israel – Abraham; Church –Christ. (6) Covenants: Israel –Abrahamic and all the following covenants; Church –indirectly related to the Abrahamic and New covenants. (7) Nationally: Israel –one nation; Church –from all nations. (8) Divine dealing: Israel –national and individual; Church –individual only. (9) Dispensations: Israel –seen in all ages from Abraham; Church – seen only in this present age. (10) Ministry: Israel –no missionary activity and no gospel to preach; Church –a commission to fulfill. (11) The death of Christ: Israel –guilty nationally, but to be saved by it; Church –perfectly saved by it now. (12) The Father: Israel –by a peculiar relationship God was Father to the nation; Church –we are related individually to God as Father. (13) Christ: Israel –Messiah, Immanuel, King; Church –Saviour, Lord, Bridegroom, Head. (14) The Holy Spirit –Israel –came upon some temporarily; Church –indwells all. (15) Governing Principle: Israel – Mosaic law system; Church –grace system. (16) Divine enablement: Israel

–none; Church – the indwelling Holy Spirit. (17) Two farewell discourses: Israel –Olivet discourse; Church –upper room discourse. (18) The promise of Christ's return: Israel –in power and glory for judgment; Church –to receive us to Himself. (19) Position: Israel–a servant; Church –members of the family. (20) Christ's earthly reign: Israel –subjects; Church –co-reigns with Christ. (21) Priesthood: Israel –had a priesthood; Church – is a priesthood. (22) Marriage: Israel –unfaithful wife; Church –bride. (23) Judgments: Israel –must face judgment; Church –delivered from all judgments. (24) Position in eternity: Israel –spirits of just men made perfect in the new earth; Church –the Church of the firstborn in the new heavens."[ii]

As one carefully studies God's Word it becomes clear that the promises given to Israel are earthly while the promises given to the Church are heavenly. Israel is by natural birth. Whereas the Church is by a supernatural birth. God's dealings with Israel have been under the Law, while His dealings with the Church are by grace. Israel, as a nation of people, began with Abraham, while the head of the Church is Christ. Israel is described as the wife of Jehovah (Isa. 54:5-8; Jer. 3:1ff). The Church is described as the bride of Christ (II Cor. 11:2; Eph. 5:23-32; Rev. 19:7-9; 21:2, 9; 22:17). Thus they are clearly two separate and distinct entities.

Understanding that the Church and Israel are two very distinct entities in Scripture will help the Bible student overcome much confusion related to the issues between the Rapture and the Second Coming. To develop any understanding of future events the student must carefully keep separated the events for Israel and the events for the Church. Recognizing this imperative, let us now consider the issue of "His appearing".

CHAPTER ONE

WHAT IS THE SECOND COMING?

What is meant by "The Second Coming"? Some suggest that the Second Coming and the Rapture are one and the same event. Others suggest that they are two events. Those who hold that they are two events disagree on the timing of the events in relation to each other. The pre-tribulationists place the Rapture before the beginning of the Tribulation. The mid-tribulationists place it at the mid point of the Tribulation. The pre-wrath position places the rapture around the sixth seal, or about six years into the Tribulation. The post tribulationist holds that the rapture occurs at the second coming with the saints meeting Him in the air before He arrives on earth. Clearly, as we shall see, the Scriptures teach that the Rapture and the Second coming of Christ are two separate events.

A Literal Bodily Coming

What is the Second Coming of Christ? First, it is a literal bodily coming. When Christ ascended into heaven after the resurrection two angels said to those present: *"Ye men of Galilee, why stand ye gazing up into heaven? This same Jesus, which is taken up from you into heaven, shall so come in like manner as ye have seen him go into heaven* (Acts 1:11).

Also, the Second Coming is a visible bodily coming. *"Behold, he cometh with clouds; and every eye shall see him, and they also which pierced him; and all kindreds of the earth shall wail because of him"* (Rev. 1:7). An Old Testament passage that speaks of Messiah's Second Coming is Zechariah 12:10. *"And I will pour upon the house of David, and upon the inhabitants of Jerusalem, the spirit of grace and of supplications: and they shall look upon me whom they have pierced, and they shall mourn for him, as one mourneth for his only son, and shall be in bitterness for him, as one is in bitterness for his firstborn.*" At His second coming He will be visible.

A Physical Return to Earth

The Second Coming speaks of Christ's physical return to earth (Acts 1:11). His departure was from the earth. His return will be to the earth. We are told the exact place to which He will come when He returns to the earth. Isaiah wrote: *"And the Redeemer shall come to Zion, and unto them that turn from transgression in Jacob, saith the LORD."* (Isa. 59:20). Also, in Zechariah 14:4 we read: *"And his feet shall stand in that day upon the Mount of Olives, which is before Jerusalem on the east."* As Jesus physically departed, so shall He physically return.

The purpose of the Second Coming

In His second coming the purpose is fourfold. He will return to complete the unconditional promises given to the Jew by His Father in the unconditional covenants given only to Israel. He will come to lift the curse upon creation. He will come to usher in the Millennial Kingdom of peace and righteousness. And He will come to seat Himself upon David's throne and rule the nations in fulfillment of ancient prophecy.

Thus His second coming will be visible and open for all to see. The purpose of His Second Coming is earthly in fulfillment of all of the covenant promises made to Abraham, Isaac, Jacob, David, and their descendents (cf. Isaiah 59:20-21; Zechariah 14:3-5; Daniel 4:13,17).

The purpose of the Second Coming affects both Jew and Gentile. First, our Lord will come to judge the nations (Matt. 25:31-32). Note the timing of this judgment: *"When the Son of man shall come in His glory…"* It would appear that one of the very first things He does is to judge the nations on the basis of how they treated His people, the nation of Israel. Though I think that a case could be made that this judgment will also include how the nations treated His people, the Church (cf. Matt. 25:35-46), the primary implication is in regard to their treatment of Israel. The phrase, "my brethren", as found in Matthew 25:40 is most often used to denote His people, the Jews. But it is also used by Jesus to denote believers (cf. Matt. 28:10). His first act, upon His second coming, is to purify the world. Only the righteous will actually enter into the Millennial Kingdom (cf. Matt. 25:34, 46). This is not the judgment of the Great White Throne described in Revelation 20:11-15. That judgment takes place at the conclusion of the Millennial Kingdom whereas this judgment of the nations takes place at the very beginning.

The Second Coming is necessary to complete the fulfillment of the unconditional promises God made to Israel through the covenants; in particular, the Davidic Covenant (II Samuel 7:12-16). This covenant not only promised David that Solomon would reign after him, but that *"thine house and thy Kingdom shall be established forever before thee; thy throne shall be established forever."* (v. 16). Note the emphasis given by the repetition of the promise of his Kingdom being established forever. God's Word consistently speaks of Messiah ruling on David's throne from Jerusalem, not only over Israel, but over the whole world (cf. Rev. 11:15; Zech 9:10; Psalm 2:8-9). The promise further states that, at this time, Israel will no longer be the tail but the head of the nations, as all nations will come to Jerusalem at least once a year to worship (cf. Zech. 14:16).

It is interesting to note at this point that Christ will rule over Israel and the nations. But the Church will rule "with" Him (cf. Rev. 2:26; II Tim. 2:12; Rev. 20:4-6).

CHAPTER TWO

WHAT IS THE RAPTURE?

Rapture is not a Biblical term. But neither is Tri-unity. Yet both represent concepts that are clearly taught in the Scriptures. According to Webster's Unabridged Dictionary the noun "rapture" means "to carry away". There is a Biblical term that means the same thing. It is the word "translate". According to Webster "translate" means to change from one place to another. It is interesting that Webster also states that it means: "to convey to heaven, originally without death."[iii]

This term is used only three times in Scripture: II Samuel 3:10; Colossians 1:13; Hebrews 11:5. In the first two instances of its usage it clearly means to move from one place to another. Hebrews speaks of the catching away of Enoch. Genesis 5:24 states: *"And Enoch walked with God: and he was not; for God took him."* The writer of Hebrews describes Enoch as a godly man whom God took to heaven (translated) without him passing through physical death. There is one other Old Testament Character who had a similar experience. That was Elijah as recorded in II Kings 2:11. Both were "translated" from earth to heaven. This is the exact sense of the context of I Thessalonians 4:16-17. Notice that the "dead in Christ" rise first. Then those who are yet alive are *"caught up together with them in the clouds..."* The word 'rapture' and the word 'translate' both mean to be removed from one place and taken to another. Though the word 'rapture' is not a Biblical term it does depict a Biblical concept. If you insist on a Biblical term the word is 'translate'. Either way, the message is clear. There is a day coming when our Lord will come for His bride (the true Church) and catch us away to meet Him in the air from whence He will carry us on to heaven. The concept of the Rapture is Biblical.

The Rapture vs. the 2nd Coming

The Rapture, or translation, describes the event when Jesus, the Bridegroom, will come for His Bride, the saints. *"For the Lord himself shall descend from heaven with a shout, with the voice of the archangel, and with the trump of God: and the dead in Christ shall rise first: Then we which are alive and remain shall be caught up together with them in the clouds, to meet the Lord in the air: and so shall we ever be with the Lord. Wherefore comfort one another with these words."* (I Thess. 4:16-18). Note that the passage is clear, that He comes only "for" His own. At the Second Coming He comes "with" the saints (cf. Jude 14; I Thess. 3:13). The Rapture for the Church is from earth to heaven. The 2nd Coming is the Church coming from heaven to earth with her Lord.

Note also that, at the Rapture, the Lord is preceded with the sound of the trumpet and the shout of the archangel. There is no such announcement preceding His Second Coming. With the Second Coming the heavens open, He appears on a white horse (cf. Rev. 19:11) and directly proceeds to come to earth.

Note further that the saints of past generations, from the beginning of the Church, are raised to meet Him in the air. The saints living at the moment of His appearing are caught up to meet Him in the air (cf. v. 17). There is no resurrection of the saints tied to His Second Coming, nor a catching away of living saints to meet Him in the air. The Rapture is a meeting in the air (in the clouds) of Christ and His true bride, the true Church.

The Second Coming is an event that is seen by all. Whereas the Rapture is secret and mysterious (cf. I Cor. 15:50-52). There is not one verse that describes the Rapture event as one that is seen by every eye. It is secret. Suddenly the saints are gone; just caught away.

The Purpose of the Rapture

The purpose of the Rapture is to finish our salvation and to present us to the Father as Christ's Holy Bride (Rom. 8:23; Eph. 5:25-27; II Cor. 11:2; Rev. 19:7). Thus the Rapture relates only to the Church. The Rapture and its purpose is to be an encouragement and comfort to the saints (I Thess. 4:18). What a comfort and encouragement it is to know that the good work He has begun in us He will one day finish to His glory. There is no comfort for the saints in the thought that they will go through any portion of God's wrath.

So, it is clear that the Rapture (Translation) and the Second Coming are not the same event. They focus on two different groups. They have two different purposes. They have completely different sets of circumstances describing them. They are two separate events. Thus, those who hold to a post-Tribulation position with the saints being caught up to meet the Lord as He descends to establish the Kingdom are wrong as must also be the amillennialists.

The Next Question

As we have established that these are two separate events, the next question that must occupy our attention is the timing of the two events. We already know that the Second Coming occurs at the conclusion of the Tribulation after Israel and the unredeemed world experience God's judgment for seven years. There is little, if any, controversy regarding this issue. Let us then turn our attention to what Scripture teaches us regarding the timing of the Rapture (Translation).

CHAPTER THREE

DANIEL 9 AND THE TRIBULATION

The area of greatest confusion among the majority who recognize that the Rapture and the Second Coming are two distinctly separate events is the timing of the Rapture. With the exception of the pre-tribulation Rapture position all the other positions have the Church going through some part of the Tribulation. So the real question is does the believing Church go through any part of the Tribulation. If it does, we must decide who is right among the different positions which have the Church going through at least some part of the Tribulation. If God's Word does not teach that the Church will go through any part of the Tribulation, the Pre-tribulation position must then be the Biblical position. Thus our task is to determine whether or not the believing Church goes through any part of the Tribulation.

The book of Daniel is a key book of prophecy in helping us to understand this matter. Essentially, the first eight chapters of Daniel deal with revelations to Daniel regarding the Gentiles. When we come to chapter nine Daniel's concern for his own people comes to the forefront. Daniel is aware of the prophecies of Jeremiah, especially the prophecy relating to the length of time for the captivity of the Jews in Babylon (cf. Dan. 9:2). He was quite aware that the time of their captivity was about to come to an end. So Daniel's question to God was: "You have told me about your plans for the Gentiles; but, God, what about my people?" At the beginning of his prayer, he confesses the sins of his people and nation and begs for God's mercy and grace (Dan. 9:3-19). His request is for deliverance and information as to what is going to happen to his people in relation to what Daniel understood was God's unconditional promises given to his forefathers. As Daniel prayed, God heard his prayer and sent

Gabriel to reveal His plans for the nation and Daniel's people as Daniel had requested. This revelation is given in verses 20 through 27.

The Seventy Weeks

First, we need to understand that this prophecy is about Daniel's people, the Jews, and the city of Jerusalem. Note what Gabriel said to Daniel as recorded in verse 24: *"Seventy weeks are determined upon thy people and upon thy holy city..."* This prophecy has to do only with the Jewish people and the Holy City. That is important for the student to understand. God goes on through Gabriel to state six issues that will be resolved during this prophetic time period.

The time frame of this prophecy is literally "seventy sevens." A study of history demonstrates that these sevens are years and that the beginning point was with the decree of Artaxerxes in 445 B.C. The key is found in verse 25. There are two qualifying factors to identify the correct decree and thus establish the correct starting point. They are: *from the going forth of the commandment to restore and to build Jerusalem."* This particular commandment has nothing to do with permission to rebuild the Temple; only with a commandment that would allow the Jews to restore and rebuild the City of Jerusalem. There were four decrees. The first decree was given by Cyrus in 536 B.C. (Ezra 1:1-4). The second decree was given by Darius in 519 B.C. and was a re-affirmation of the decree of Cyrus (cf. Ezra 5:1-6:12). The third decree was given by Artaxerxes in 458 B.C. The fourth decree issued in 445 B.C. was also given by Artaxerxes authorizing Nehemiah to return to his homeland for the express purpose of restoring and rebuilding the Holy City (cf. Neh. 2:1-8). The first three decrees relate specifically to the Temple. Only the last decree relates to the restoration and rebuilding of the Holy City. So the starting point of this prophecy must be 445 B.C.

In this prophecy there are 69 sevens from the decree to the cutting off of the Messiah. After researching the matter Sir Robert Anderson came to the conclusion that the decree was issued on March 14, 445 B.C. Computing with a lunar year (360 days), the Biblical reckoning of time, the total days for the 483 years is 173,880 days which brings us to April 6, 32 A.D., the day that Jesus presented Himself to the nation as their Messiah/King.[iv] At that time He was rejected, and a few days later, crucified (cut off) fulfilling this point of the prophecy.

God informs Daniel that He has a six-fold purpose to be accomplished for Israel and the Jewish people over these prophesied 490 years. First, He states the purpose to be: *"to finish the transgression."* The word translated 'transgression' is "pasha" which literally means to rebel against proper authority. Israel's greatest sin has been their rebellion against God's rule. Because of this rebellion Israel continues to refuse to repent, turn to God and receive Yeshua as their Saviour and King. Unfortunately, there will not be a national repentance until the Second Coming of their Messiah which concludes the final week of these prophetic years. Sadly, according to Zechariah 13:8-9 only one third of the Jewish population in Israel and, according to Ezekiel 20:33-38, only one tenth of the Jews that have not returned to the Promised Land, will survive the Tribulation long enough to recognize Yeshua for who he is, repent of their unbelief and receive Him as their Messiah/King.

Second, God states the purpose to be: *"to make an end of sins".* These are the daily sins that result from their rebellion. Nationally, there will be no end of this until Yeshua comes the second time. Third, this period of time is set aside *"to make reconciliation for iniquity".* One issue that will be resolved during this time frame will be the atoning sacrifice of Christ at His first coming. Apart from His atoning work there is no hope for the nation (cf Hebrews 10). Fourth, another matter to be concluded during this time frame is *"to bring in everlasting righteousness".* Every change among Daniel's people necessary to establish a lasting righteousness must be accomplished in preparation for the coming of their eternal King.

Fifth, Gabriel states that the purpose of this period is *"to seal up the vision and prophecy."* "Seal up" denotes to confirm, ratify, authenticate for fulfillment. Thus, all prophecy that is fulfilled will no longer be of concern. The visions and prophecies here spoken of are those that have proclaimed Israel's chastening because of their rebellion and resulting sins. When they have repented of their sins and received by faith the atoning sacrifice of their Messiah King these visions and prophecies will be sealed never to be opened again. Finally, Gabriel said that the purpose of this time period was *"to anoint the Most Holy".* This, in all probability, denotes the anointing of the Millennial Temple area for holy service. The Temple and its service are described in Ezekiel 40-48. Ezekiel 43:12 states: *"This is the law of the house; upon the top of the mountain round about shall be most holy. Behold, this is the law of the house."* This requirement will be fulfilled at the conclusion of Daniel's prophecy when the Messiah returns the second time to establish the Millennial Kingdom. Thus we learn that the tribulation period, by definition, is the final seven years of God's dealings with Daniel's people and the Holy City, to finish Israel's transgression, to end Israel's sins and to make reconciliation for Israel's iniquity. This prophecy relates solely to Israel, Daniel's people. There is no purpose in the Tribulation, as stated here, for the Church, as the church is nowhere mentioned in the Old Testament.

Further, note that there is a parenthetic period between the fulfillment of the first 69 weeks (483 years) and the beginning of the 70th week (the last 7 years). First, there are several years (38 years) from Messiah being cut off and the prophesied destruction of the City and the Temple. We are told that this act of destruction would be accomplished by the people out of whom would later come a Prince who would make a seven year peace pact with Israel (cf. v. 27). This destruction of the City and Temple was accomplished in 70 A.D. by the Romans. After a study of other related Old Testament passages and the Book of the Revelation, it is clear that the 70th week (7 year period) is what is described as the Tribulation Period. In the Hebrew Scriptures (OT) this is also known as the Day of the Lord (cf. Joel 1:15, etc). So, this 70th week of Daniel's prophecy is the final prophecy of judgment upon Israel to prepare them for their coming King and the establishment of the Millennial Kingdom. To date 69 of the seventy sevens have been completed. We know that to be a fact. Verse 26 of the prophecy speaks of Messiah's first coming, His vicarious atonement and the destruction of the Temple and the City. This has already occurred. The verse reads: *"And after three score and two weeks Messiah shall be cut off, but not for Himself; and the people of the prince that shall come shall destroy the city and the sanctuary; and the end thereof shall be with a flood and unto the end of the war desolations are determined."*

The parenthetic period between the 69th week and the 70th week is where the Church Age (the Age of Grace) has been inserted by God. Why the insertion of the Age of Grace? God's purpose for Israel, among other things, was to be the repository of His revelation and then they were to share that revelation with the world. They received and faithfully recorded the revelations of God. But they failed to share them with the world. We usually think of Jonah as emphasizing Missions. And so it does. But the real story is the account of the prophet, Jonah, who is commissioned by God to take the good news to Nineveh and share it with the Gentiles living there who were perceived by Jonah as Israel's enemy. Thus, he did not want to go. He knew that they would repent and that God would be gracious to them. He did not want that. Jonah exemplified the attitude of Israel in their unwillingness to share God's revelation with a lost world. So God temporarily set them (the nation) aside. Because God's redemptive plan included Gentiles as well as Jews He inserted the Church Age in this parenthetic period before the final curtain was drawn on His dealings with National Israel (cf. Rom 11:11, 30,31) so that Gentiles would have the opportunity to hear and receive the gospel and, in turn, take the gospel back to the Jews. As the Church Age is a period of time during which God has stopped dealing with Israel and the Jew nationally for the express purpose of calling out a people for His Name that will include both individual Jews and Gentiles, though He will again deal with the Jews nationally with the beginning of the fulfillment of the final week of this prophecy, it only follows that the true believing Church, having completed its Divine purpose, will be removed before the beginning of the final act of God's dealings with national Israel. There is no stated purpose for the Church in the 70th week of Daniel's prophecy, nor anywhere else. Thus, there is no reason for the believing Church to remain here to pass through this time of judgment.

Those who would have the Church going through any part of the Tribulation believe that the Church has failed. So they believe that God can be just only if the Church is punished for her sins. This is their argument. That would be true except that, for the believer (the true Church), Christ died for their sins, all of them, past, present and future! However, the institutional Church, which is made up of unbelievers, will go into and through the Tribulation and will be judged (cf. Rev. 18). The Bible demands that we make this distinction between the believing (true) Church and the institutional Church.

The prophecy of Daniel 9 precludes the true Church from any participation in the fulfillment of this final week of prophecy that relates only to Israel and Daniel's people.

CHAPTER FOUR

THE RAPTURE AND OTHER OLD TESTAMENT INDICATORS

One accepted principle of interpretation is the fact that things in the Old Testament often establish patterns. That is certainly true in relation to God's dealings with His creation. As the Rapture is only an issue that relates to the Church, and as the Church is only found in the New Testament and not in the Old Testament, the Rapture *per se* is not found in the Old Testament. However, patterns of how God acts in certain circumstances are established in the Old Testament that enables us to understand what He is doing in the New Testament. One pattern which is established in the Old Testament is how God deals with the righteous in times when He is preparing to judge the unrighteous when the righteous and unrighteous are intermingled. The purpose of this chapter is to demonstrate that such a pattern is clearly established in the Old Testament.

One of the issues before us in this study is how God deals with the righteous in the light of the prophesied outpouring of His judgment on the unrighteous. The overwhelming majority of Bible scholars agree that the Tribulation is a prophesied time for the outpouring of God's wrath upon an evil and sinful people, both Jewish and Gentile. Dr. S. Franklin Logsdon gave the clearest Biblical definition of the Tribulation when he wrote: "The Tribulation period is the final seven years of God's determined dealings with Daniel's people and the holy city, to finish Israel's transgression, to end Israel's sins and to make reconciliation for Israel's iniquity (Dan. 9:24)."ᵛ The Tribulation is clearly a time of divine judgment. Does the Old Testament establish a divine pattern regarding His treatment of the righteous immediately preceding the outpouring of divine judgment or wrath upon the unrighteous? If such a pattern is established it gives us valuable information for determining the timing of the Rapture.

Noah

God's dealing with Noah establishes a pattern. Noah was a righteous man (Gen. 6:9). When God was about to judge the earth he called Noah, informed him of what He was going to do, and instructed him to build an ark as a place of safety from the judgment about to fall. God separated the righteous from the unrighteous before the judgment fell.

Abraham and Lot

Beginning in Genesis 18:16 we have the account of God revealing to Abraham His plans to destroy Sodom and Gomorrah. Abraham knows that Lot and his family are dwelling there so he bargains with God. *"And Abraham drew near, and said, Wilt thou also destroy the righteous with the wicked?"* (Gen. 18:23). Herein is the principle established. Will God destroy the righteous with the wicked? The ensuing verses give us the answer. God agrees not to destroy Sodom and Gomorrah if there are at least ten righteous people there.

But there were less than ten. In Genesis chapter nineteen we have the record of God sending two angels to warn Lot of the impending judgment. Lot prepares to flee and the angels instruct them to hurry. *"Haste thee, escape thither; for I cannot do anything till thou be come thither."* (Gen. 19:22). Clearly, God had determined that He would not pour out His judgment upon Sodom and Gomorrah until all the righteous were removed to a place of safety. This is the second time God functioned on this basis. The first was His removal of Noah and his family into a place of safety before He poured out His judgment upon the earth. A pattern is clearly established. In the face of imminent massive judgment God removes the righteous to a place of safety.

The Wilderness Wanderings

In Numbers 16 we have two accounts of how God dealt with the righteous when planning to pour out His wrath upon those who had grievously sinned. The first is the rebellion of Korah recorded in Numbers 16:1-35. In verse 21 God instructs Moses and Aaron to separate themselves from the congregation whom He was about to consume. Moses and Aaron plead for the congregation. In verse 26 the congregation was instructed to separate themselves from "these wicked men", that is from Korah and those who followed him. Those who separated were not judged. Those who stood with Korah were swallowed up with all of their possessions when the earth opened.

In Numbers 16:41 ff the congregation again rebelled against God's man, Moses. God spoke to Moses instructing him to: *"Get you up from among this congregation, that I may consume them in a moment"* (v. 45). Moses and Aaron immediately began to pray before the Lord and took action to provide atonement for the sins of the congregation. But 14,700 died of the plague before the plague was stayed. Note that God separated the righteous from the sinners to be judged before His judgment fell. A principle is established that follows through the Bible in God's dealings with His world.

Understanding the Rapture to occur before the Tribulation, the outpouring of God's wrath, is in agreement with the principle established early in God's dealings with His creation. It establishes God's sense of justice. For the true believing Church to go through any part of the Tribulation flies in the face of a clearly established pattern of God's dealings in these situations.

Other Indicators

Consider other indicators of the same pattern. We have already noted that the concept of the Rapture was clearly depicted in the catching away (rapture) of Enoch and the prophet Elijah. There are also at least two other Old Testament passages that clearly picture the concept.

Isaiah 26:19-21

The verses immediately preceding this passage deal with the issue of resurrection. Verse 14 speaks of the unrighteous dead. Death, by definition, is simply separation. Physical death is the separation of the soul and spirit from the body. Spiritual death is the separation of man from

God. Consider the example of Adam and Eve in the garden. At the outset, God walked and communed with them daily. But when they sinned, that relationship was lost. After God had placed Adam in the garden and given him oversight of all that was there, He told him that he could eat of every fruit except the fruit of the tree of the knowledge of good and evil. He was warned that to disobey would result in death (Gen 2:16, 17). First, their disobedience resulted in the loss of their relationship with God (Gen. 3:8). They immediately died a spiritual death that was later followed by their physical death. Paul, in his epistle to the Romans wrote: *"For the wages of sin is death."* (Rom. 6:23). The unrighteous dead are forever separated from God, first in Hades, and then later in the Lake of Fire (cf. Rev. 20:11-15).

In the passage under consideration, Verse 19 speaks of the death of believers, of the faithful and their resurrection from physical death to live eternally in the presence of their God. This resurrection is depicted as a joyous and glorious occurrence.

Verse 20 is an invitation to the faithful to come and be hidden (protected) for a brief time until *"the indignation be overpast."* Verse 21 establishes the time element for all of this by describing the time when God will come to punish *"the inhabitants of the earth for their iniquities".* That is the Tribulation or Daniel's 70th week of years. Thus this "hiding" of the believers immediately precedes the time of great Divine judgment. Peter Steveson, in his commentary on Isaiah writes: "Isaiah 26:19-21 gives a graphic picture of the pre-tribulation rapture of believers. Verse 19 describes the resurrection of the dead bodies, plural, not singular as in the AV. The Lord's invitation to His people is to 'hide.....until the indignation is past,' v. 20. Verse 21 completes this brief thought by giving the reason for the Rapture. The Lord hides His people from His punishment of the wicked earth."[vi] He later states: "Until the passing of the indignation, the Tribulation, the saints will enter into their 'chambers.' They will stay there for 'a little moment' until the ending of the 'indignation.' The picture is of the saints, sheltered in heaven during the tribulation on earth, v. 20."[vii]

Zephaniah 2:1-3

This is another interesting passage that clearly suggests a pre-tribulation rapture. Notice two things from verse 1. The Hebrew word translated "nation" is "goy" or "goyim" which means Gentile or heathen. Notice further, that this is a people "not desired". Matthew Henry states: "The word signifies either, 1. *Not desiring,* that they have no desire towards God. Or, 2. *Not desirable,* not having anything that might recommend them to God".[viii]

This is a call to examine one's self to determine one's sins so that you may confess them and do what needs to be done to get right with your God. According to verse 2 they are encouraged to do this *"before the day of the LORD's anger come upon you."* The Day of the LORD is another term describing Daniel's 70th week, the Tribulation Period when God will pour out His wrath (anger) upon all who refuse to believe.

The stated motive for the examination and getting right with God is that *"it may be ye shall be hid in the day of the LORD's anger."* The thought here is precisely the same as we find in Isaiah 26:20. Once again we have a reference to a deliverance of the faithful "before" the beginning of "The Day of the LORD", or the Tribulation.

This pattern is established in the catching away of Enoch and Elijah which are types of the Rapture, in the issue of Sodom and Gomorrah, and in the teaching of the prophets Isaiah and Zephaniah. As a pattern of how God deals with the righteous in times when He plans to judge the unrighteous is clearly established in the Old Testament, it appears that Old Testament typology points to a pre-tribulation catching away of the saints to deliver and protect them from the judgment of the pouring out of His wrath upon sinful, rebellious man. That understanding conforms to God's pattern established in the Old Testament record.

CHAPTER FIVE

THE CHURCH AND THE TRIBULATION

What does God's Word have to say about the Church passing through the Tribulation? The Tribulation is the outpouring of God's wrath (cf. Ezek. 7:19; Zeph. 7:14-19; Rev. 6:16, 17; 14:8-11, 19-20; 15:1, 7; 16:1, 19; 19:15). God's wrath is poured out upon man because of his sins. Consider the words of Paul as recorded in Romans 5:8, 9. *"But God commendeth his love toward us, in that, while we were yet sinners, Christ died for us. Much more then, being now justified by his blood, we shall be saved from wrath through him."* Paul wrote to the Thessalonians: *"For they themselves show of us what manner of entering in we had unto you, and how ye turned to God from idols to serve the living and true God; And to wait for his Son from heaven, whom he raised from the dead, even Jesus, which delivered us from the wrath to come."* (I Thess. 1:10). Again Paul wrote: *"For God hath not appointed us to wrath, but to obtain salvation by our Lord Jesus Christ."* (I Thess. 5:9).

First, note in the Romans passage that because we are justified by the blood of Christ we are *"saved from wrath."* This is a promise that when we accept Christ as our Saviour we are no longer subject to God's wrath. Paul speaks of this as a completed transaction. He states: *"Therefore being justified by faith, we have peace with God through our Lord Jesus Christ."* (Rom. 5:1). Paul reaffirms it in Romans 8:30, I Cor. 6:11 and I Thess. 1:10. I Thess. 5:9 simply reaffirms that deliverance from God's wrath is a result of being saved. The believer's sins were all judged at the cross. If Christ died for all of our sins, past, present and future, can God be just in judging and punishing the believer for the sins already paid for by the blood of His Son? (cf. Rom. 10:4; Jn. 19:30). Would God be just to inflict a second judgment on sin already judged at the cross and only on the few who happen to be alive at the time of the beginning of the Tribulation? Perhaps He would be just in the Old Testament economy where atonement is a covering. But in the New Testament atonement denotes sins totally removed to never be held against the believer again (cf. Heb. 10:9-14). For the true believing Church to go through any part of the Tribulation for the purpose of experiencing God's wrath because of their sins would be unjust. Therefore, if God is truly righteous, the true Church must be delivered from the Tribulation. The Rapture must occur before the Tribulation begins because the Tribulation is God's judgment of the sin of unbelieving Israel and the world, not of the believing Church.

But, if this is true of the Church saints it must also be true of the Tribulation saints, some will say. The only thing that is true of the Tribulation saints is that they are saved by faith in Christ's sacrifice on Calvary. Remember, the Rapture concludes the Church Age. God moves on to conclude His dealings with Israel and His judgment of an evil world. The fact that any are saved during such calamitous times is an act of God's undeserving grace. Speaking of the martyred tribulation saints the angel said: *"These are they which came out of great tribulation, and have washed their robes, and made them white in the blood of the lamb."* (Rev. 7:14). As a matter of fact, their martyrdom will be a divine release from God's wrath, an act of God's grace. What relates to the believer in the Church Age no more relates to the believer in the Tribulation than what related to the believer before the Church Age relates to the Church Age believer. God has always dealt with each group uniquely according to His Grace.

The Location of the Church

As one studies Revelation chapters 4 to the end of the Epistle there is no mention of the believing Church on the earth as there is in Revelation chapters 2-3. There are multitudes, both Jewish and Gentile, saved during the Tribulation but they are called Tribulation Saints (cf. Rev. 7:13, 14), but not one mention of a believing Church. The Tribulation Saints are martyred for their faith. If the believing Church did enter into some portion of the Tribulation they would all be martyred (cf. Rev. 7:14). So there would be no one left to rapture. For this reason alone the Rapture must take place before the inception of the Tribulation.

Revelation chapters two and three speak of the Church. But, as chapter four begins, the Church is in heaven and never again spoken of on earth. The Church Age comes to its conclusion with the Rapture, when it is caught away into heaven.

The Judgment Seat of Christ

There are at least two major events that must occur for the believing Church between the Rapture and the Second Coming. The first is the Judgment Seat of Christ. This is predicted in Romans 14:10 and II Cor. 5:10. Both passages make it clear that all Church Age believers will face this judgment. Paul, in II Cor. 5:10, states the purpose for this judgment: *"that every man may receive the things done in his body, according to that he hath done, whether it be good or bad."* The word translated "good" is from the Greek word "agathos" which is good in the sense of it being beneficial. The Greek word translated "bad" is "kakos" and is bad in the sense that it is worthless. Thus this judgment will determine the worth or lack thereof of the deeds done in the body from the day believers were saved to the day they either died or were raptured. The believer's sins were judged at the cross. Thus there can be no judgment of sin here.

This judgment is more fully described by Paul in I Cor. 3:9-15. In verse 13 we read: *"Every man's work will be made manifest: for the day shall declare it, because it shall be revealed by fire; and the fire shall try every man's work of what sort it is."* The Greek word translated "sort" is "hopoyos" and literally means character or quality. It is interesting that the six standards listed here can actually be put into two categories: those that will survive the fire and those that won't (cf. v. 12).

Do we have any clue as to what the criteria will be for this judgment? I think that Jesus, Himself, gave the criteria in a discussion with His disciples recorded in John 14. Note that in verse 15 He says: *"If ye love me keep my commandments."* In verse 21 He said: *"He that hath my commandments and keepeth them, he it is that loveth me."* And note also his words recorded in verse 23: "If a man love me he will keep my words." The criteria is going to be the motive that moved us to do (or not do) what we did while in the body. It is important to note that the Greek word translated "love" throughout this chapter is "agapao" which literally means "unconditional love". If you want to understand the character or true quality of a deed look at the motive behind it. That is precisely what Christ is going to do at this judgment!

The purpose of this judgment has nothing to do with salvation. That was settled at Calvary. It has everything to do with rewarding those who have faithfully and sacrificially served Him. *"If any man's work abide.... he shall receive a reward. If any man's work shall be burned, he shall suffer loss: but he himself shall be saved; yet so as by fire."* (I Cor. 3:14, 15). The rewards will be crowns which the saints will cast before the throne of the Lamb. We are told of five possible crowns that we could receive. In I Cor. 9:25 we are told of an Incorruptible Crown. This crown will be given to those who gain mastery over their old nature. In I Thess. 2:19 we see the potential for a Crown of Rejoicing. This is the soul winner's crown. In II Tim. 4:8 there is the possibility of a Crown of Righteousness. This crown is for all those who look and long for our Lord's appearing. There is also a Crown of Life spoken of in James 1:12. This crown is for those who endure trials because of their faith. The final crown is described in I Peter 5:4 and is a Crown of Glory. Many would say that only pastors, preachers, and missionaries have a shot at this crown, but that is not true. Anyone who buys up opportunities to teach the saints, to help other believers understand God's Word, and encourages others to walk faithfully in His will have an opportunity to receive this crown.

What will we do with these crowns? We learn what will be done with the crowns in Rev. 4:10, 11. *"The four and twenty elders fall down before him that sat on the throne, and worship him that liveth for ever and ever, and cast their crowns before the throne, saying, Thou art worthy, O Lord, to receive glory and honor and power: for thou hast created all things, and for thy pleasure they are and were created."* They will be cast before the throne of the Lamb who alone is worthy. We will recognize that, if there was any good done in our life, it was because of Him and the indwelling Holy Spirit that gave us the enablement (Acts 1:8). Thus He alone is worthy of this honor and glory. If the Church were to go through any part of the Tribulation there would be no time for the Judgment Seat events including any time for the casting of the crowns before His feet! What an embarrassment it will be to those who will have no crowns to cast at His feet. One of the reasons so often given by those who believe the Church should go through at least some portion of the Tribulation is to set out a motivation for godly living by threatening folk with the judgment of God's wrath in the Tribulation. How sad, if this were the case, as only the Church that lives at the time of the Tribulation would be punished, not the Church that has existed for more than two thousand years preceding the Tribulation. Surely that is neither fair nor just. As one studies the Scripture the clear difference between the Old Testament economy and the New Testament economy is the motivation to do right. Under the law the motivation is fear of judgment. Under grace it is God's unconditional love for the sinner. The Church going through any part of the Tribulation does not fit the profile of the Age of Grace.

The Marriage of the Lamb

The second event for the Church is the Marriage of the Lamb. In the Old Testament God uses marriage as a figure of spiritual relationships. It speaks of Israel as the wife of Jehovah. The prophets often spoke of her as an unfaithful wife violating her marriage vows (cf. Isa. 54:1-17; Hosea 2:1-23; etc). The New Testament establishes an interesting and unique relationship between the Church and Christ. It describes Christ as the bridegroom and the Church as His bride awaiting the coming of her husband to whom she is betrothed (cf. John 3:29; Rom. 7:4; II Cor. 11:2; Eph. 5:25-27, 32; Rev. 19:7-8). To understand this relationship, it is important that we understand the Jewish marriage customs of the day. There are four stages: the betrothal; the fetching of the bride; the marriage ceremony; and the marriage supper.

The betrothal involved the establishment of the marriage covenant (Ketuba) and the paying of the dowry. Just as the Jewish bridegroom took the initiative by leaving his father's house to go to the home of his prospective bride, so Jesus left His Father's house in heaven and traveled to earth over two thousand years ago for the purpose of obtaining His bride, through the establishment of a covenant (Phil 2:5-8). On the same night in which Jesus made His promise recorded in John 14:1-3 He instituted what we know as the Lord's Supper. Taking the cup He said: *"This is my blood of the New Testament (New Covenant) which is shed for many for the remission of sins."* (Matt. 26:28). Just as the bride confirmed her participation in the betrothal by also drinking of the cup, so we today re-confirm our covenant relationship with Christ as we drink of that cup. As the Jewish groom paid a price for his bride, so Christ paid a price for His bride, the Church (cf. I Cor. 6:20; 7:22-23; Col. 1:18-22). As the Jewish bride was set apart (sanctified) exclusively for her groom, so is the believer declared to be sanctified (set apart) unto Christ. (cf. I Cor. 1:2; 6:11; Heb. 10:10). As the Jewish groom left the bride's home and returned to his father's house after establishment of the marriage covenant for the purpose of preparing a home for his new bride, so Christ returned to His Father's house to prepare for His bride a home. (Cf. John 14:1-2; 20:17; Col. 3:1; Heb. 1:3).

The Church is now living in that period of separation. While the bridegroom is preparing a home, the bride is to be about the business of preparing for the great day of His return to take her home to ever be with Him. As the groom ultimately comes at the end of this period of separation and preparation, so Christ will one day soon come for His Church (John 14:3). Just as the Jewish bride did not know the exact time of the groom's coming, the Church does not know the exact time of Christ's return. Thus we are to live in the expectancy of His return at any moment (I John 3:2-3) as did the betrothed bride.

The coming of the bridegroom to get his bride and take her to his father's home precedes the marriage ceremony. This ceremony is recorded in Rev. 19:6-8. We may also note the timing of this ceremony by the context. Rev. 19:1-10 describes events preceding the Second Coming. Verses eleven to twenty -one of chapter nineteen describe the Second Coming. So the Marriage must take place after the Judgment Seat of Christ and precede the Second Coming of Christ. It is also to be noted that when Christ returns He returns "with" the saints (cf. Zech. 14:5). Rev. 19:14 describes the saints as "the armies which were in heaven." Oliver B. Green stated: "The riders of the white horses were clothed in fine linen, white and clean. This is the heavenly attire of the saints that make up the Bride. It is clear that the Bride will accompany Christ when He returns to earth."[ix]

These events for the believing Church take place in heaven. The Judgment Seat of Christ occurs immediately after the Rapture and before the beginning of the Tribulation (cf. Rev. 4:1-4) while the marriage occurs just before our Lord's Second Coming. If the Church is in heaven from the Judgment Seat of Christ through the marriage ceremony, there is no room for the Church to go through any part of the Tribulation.

The fourth step of the Jewish Marriage process is the Marriage Supper. The marriage involves only the Church. The Marriage Supper involves the Church as Christ's Bride, plus resurrected Old Testament and Tribulation saints who are the friends of the Bridegroom (cf. Matt. 22:1-14; 25:1-13). Revelation 19:9 gives us the invitation to the Marriage Supper. The Marriage Supper will take place at the beginning of the Millennium after Christ returns with the Church at His Second Coming (cf. Matt. 24:42-25:13).

Conclusions

As the marriage must occur after the Judgment Seat of Christ and before the Second Coming and, as both of these events take place in heaven during the Tribulation, the Rapture must occur before the Tribulation.

CHAPTER SIX

THE REVELATION OF THE ANTICHRIST

Another issue that must be considered as we seek to determine the timing of the Rapture is the issue of when, in relation to the Rapture, is the antichrist revealed. It is clear that the appearance of the antichrist precipitates the beginning of the Tribulation (cf. Daniel 9:26-27; II Thess. 2:1-17), not the Rapture. Will the true Church still be here when he is revealed? If the answer is 'yes' then the Church will go through at least some part of the Tribulation. If the answer is 'no' then the true Church must be caught away before the beginning of the Tribulation.

II Thessalonians 2:1-12

The key passage regarding the revealing of the antichrist is II Thessalonians 2. False teachers had moved the Thessalonians to believe that the Tribulation had already begun. There were some who were teaching that the trials and persecutions the believers were experiencing indicated that they were already in the Tribulation. Paul writes this epistle to help the believers understand that the Day of the Lord had not yet begun.

Paul teaches them that there are two events that will occur immediately preceding the Tribulation. *"Let no man deceive you by any means: for that day shall not come, except there come a falling away first, and that the man of sin be revealed, the son of perdition."* (II Thess. 2:3). The first event of which Paul speaks is the coming of a day when there will be a great falling away. The Greek word translated 'falling away' is 'apostasia' or apostasy. The article 'the' denotes a very specific apostasy that will occur before the revealing of the man of sin here spoken of. Apostasy is the abandonment of the true faith. Indeed, we are seeing more and more of that in these days in which we are presently living. We are quick to point fingers at what is known today as liberal Christianity who have already turned their back on the fundamentals of the faith. But are we not also seeing within fundamental and evangelical circles the effects of compromise both in doctrine and practice? We are truly living in the day of a lukewarm Church. But there are still some that are faithful. The word here is the same as the Hebrew word found in Jeremiah 28:16 where it literally means "rebellion against the LORD". This is exactly what Peter was talking about when he warned against apostate teachers (II Peter 2:1-3). This apostasy will be a total turning from the truth and the embracing of the false religion of the great whore of Revelation 17. That cannot occur until the true Church is taken out of the way.

Along with this great apostasy will be the rise of a man who will have no respect for truth or lawfulness. He will be a man who will go beyond self exaltation and envision himself as God, the one who can truly do no wrong (cf. II Thess. 2:4). Paul's argument is that, as these events have not yet occurred, one can be assured one is not in the Great Tribulation.

Paul goes on to tell us that these events cannot occur until something else happens. *"For the mystery of iniquity doth already work: only he who letteth will let, until he be taken out of the way. And then shall that wicked be revealed…"* (vv. 7, 8a). The Greek word translated 'letteth' and 'let' is the same word, 'katecho', which literally means "to restrain". A more understandable translation would be: "only he who now restrains will restrain." Who is identified in Scripture as the restrainer? We are given a clue in Genesis 6:3. *And the LORD said: "My spirit shall not always strive with man…"* God's activity relating to Job establishes a good example as He restrains Satan from doing all that he wanted to do to Job. Some find support from Isa. 59:19 where God restrains Israel's enemies. There are many other illustrations in the Old Testament of God guiding His people through the power of the Holy Spirit restraining sin and rebellion. Some have suggested that the restrainer is human government. However, human government continues to exist into and throughout the Tribulation. Paul instructs us that the restrainer will be removed before the Tribulation can begin. (II Thess. 2:7)

Where does the Holy Spirit reside today? Does He not reside in the believer, the true Church? The moment one trusts in Christ for salvation he is indwelt by the Holy Spirit (Acts 1:8; I Cor. 12:13, etc.). The believer is thus baptized into one body, the Church. In the Old Testament economy the Holy Spirit came and went as God needed people empowered for ministry. Only in the Church Age are believers permanently indwelt. If the Holy Spirit indwells believers (the true Church), the antichrist cannot be revealed until the true Church is removed as there is no passage that teaches the removal during the Church Age of the Holy Spirit from the believer after the believer is indwelt.

If the antichrist cannot be revealed until the Holy Spirit is removed and the Holy Spirit indwells the Church (true believers), then the Tribulation cannot begin until the Church is removed to allow the coming of the antichrist. This clearly necessitates a pre-tribulation Rapture.

CHAPTER SEVEN

IS THE CATCHING AWAY IMMINENT?

Does the Bible teach that the Rapture is imminent, that it will occur without preconditions or warning? Again, if the Bible teaches that the catching away of the true Church is imminent, then only the pre -tribulation position can be the right position. Most of those holding the other views on the timing of the Rapture would agree with the forgoing statement. Let us move forward by seeking to determine what the Scriptures teach on this matter of immanency.

The Church in the Gospels

Bob Shelton, in his book entitled "God's Prophetic Blueprint" suggests that it is not signs that the believers are to look for, but sounds. He states: "the so-called signs of the times, even those of Matthew 24, are not events that must precede the Rapture of the Church. They are signs to those who will be living in Tribulation days that point to the return of Christ in His Revelation."ˣ One great error made by many today is to apply prophetic truth found in the Gospels to the church when, in reality, most of it applies to the unbelieving world as is all this hype regarding the "blood moons".

There are only two passages in the four Gospels where the term "church" is even used. The first is found in Matthew 16:18-19. The Greek word translated "church" simply means "a called out assembly." To the Greek it suggested a self-governing, democratic society. To the Jew of Jesus' day it suggested a theocratic society whose members were subjects of the heavenly King. It is the Jewish concept that is used here by Jesus. The "rock" of which Jesus speaks in verse 16 is the confession that Jesus is the Christ, the Son of the living God; that He is both Messiah and diety. So Jesus proclaims that a society of believers will be established. Nothing in these verses addresses end time issues.

The second usage of the term is found in Matthew 18:15-20 and simply addresses the issue of how to deal with sin among believers. Again, these verses do not address end time issues. Nowhere in the Gospels is there given any prophecies relating to signs for the Church that must be fulfilled before the Church can be removed.

Cogent New Testament Texts

It must be stated up front that there is not any Scripture that simply states that our Lord's return is imminent. However, Scripture does establish an attitude of expectancy for our Lord's imminent return to catch away His bride. In John 14:2-3 Jesus promises that He will return for His bride, the Church. When this passage is taken in the context of the Jewish marriage customs of the time it clearly indicates that there are no signs for which the bride is to watch which must be fulfilled before the Bridegroom can come.

There is no sign given for which we must look for fulfillment before His return for the saints. In his description of the resurrection of the saints as recorded in I Cor. 15:51-52 the resurrection occurs suddenly and without warning. There are no signs preceding it.

The Church is admonished to look for His coming (cf. Phil. 3:20; Titus 2:13). In I Cor. 1:7 and I Thess. 1:10 the Church is called to wait for His coming. His implied imminent return is given to be a strong motive for His children to live godly lives (cf. I Cor. 4:5 which speaks of the Bema seat judgment which occurs after the Rapture; Col. 3:4; I Tim. 6:14; I Jn. 2:28). None of these passages give even a hint that there is anything that must be fulfilled before He returns for His bride. His imminent return is strongly implied.

In Rev. 3:11; 22:7, 12, 20 He says: *"Behold, I come quickly."* Dr. Renald Showers, commenting on these statements wrote: "Through these assertions Christ intended to do two things: arouse the attention of Christians to the fact that His coming could happen at any moment; and give believers solemn assurance of the fulfillment of His promise of His imminent return."[xi] Do you not find it interesting that not even Jesus, Himself, says: "After certain things occur, then I will come quickly"?

There are two other references that also imply the imminent return of our Lord. In Phil. 4:5 Paul states: *"Let your moderation be known unto all men. The Lord is at hand."* Paul indicates here that the Lord could return at any moment. That is what is meant by imminent. The other reference is found in I John 5:8. *"Be ye also patient, stablish your hearts: for the coming of the Lord draweth nigh."* Again, the implication is that the Lord could return at any moment and this should motivate one to godly living.

Conclusions

There are three conclusions we may draw from this study. Signs were given to Israel that would precede the Second Coming to motivate them to get their house in order. This has nothing to do with the Church. In order to understand Scripture correctly we must keep Israel and the Church separate. Is the Scripture incomplete because there is not one verse that admonishes or commands the Church to look for and wait for the fulfillment of a sign to indicate His coming for His bride? I understand that this is an argument from silence. But this silence is deafening in the light of the importance of this issue and the strong evidence indicating an attitude of imminent expectancy. Finally, there is an overwhelming amount of Scripture that establishes the necessity for the attitude of expectancy for the imminent return of the Lord establishing a strong and clear motive for godly living while we wait.

I like the statement made by Dr. Showers when he wrote: "The concept of the imminent coming of Christ strongly infers a pre-tribulation Rapture of the Church and therefore is significant evidence in favor of that view."[xii]

CHAPTER EIGHT

THE LAST TRUMP

Before we conclude this study there is one other issue we need to consider. For many there is some confusion about what Paul meant when he wrote: *"Behold, I show you a mystery; We shall not all sleep, but we shall all be changed, In a moment, in the twinkling of an eye, at the last trump: for the trumpet shall sound, and the dead shall be raised incorruptible ,and we shall be changed."* I Corinthians 15:51-52.

The confusion surrounds the phrase: "the last trump." Some have connected this phrase to the trumpets spoken of in Revelation Chapter eight and use it as an argument against the pre-tribulation rapture. There are, however, several problems with that interpretation.

THE PROBLEMS

The first problem is that Paul wrote the Corinthian Epistles approximately 30 years <u>before</u> John wrote the Revelation. So there is no way there could be a connection between what Paul wrote and what John wrote in Revelation chapter eight.

The second problem for those wanting to make this connection is that Paul, in I Thessalonians 4:16, 17 describes this trumpet as the "trump of God." In Revelation 8:2 these trumpets are blown by seven angels: *"And I saw the seven angels which stood before God; and to them were given seven trumpets."* As you read the rest of chapter eight and also chapter nine it is clear that these trumpets are sounded by angels. In Revelation 11:15 we read: *"And the seventh angel sounded..."* According to Revelation 10:7 the mystery of God is finished. This trumpet will take history to the end of the revelation of both God's wrath and glory. The trumpets of Revelation are prophesied to be sounded by angels; whereas Paul makes clear that the "last" trump will be sounded by God Himself.

The third problem for those who want to make a connection for "the last trump" with the trumpets of Revelation 8 is that the seven trumpets in Revelation, when sounded, all bring judgment upon the earth. In I Corinthians 15:52 and I Thessalonians 4:16 the trumpet brings deliverance. As the results are so totally opposite they cannot be made to be the same.

THE SOLUTION

What, then, is meant by the phrase "the last trump"? This was an expression very familiar to the people of Paul's day and to Paul. It was a commonly used command in the Roman army of the day. When a camp was to be broken up a trumpet sounded. The first blast meant to "strike your tents and prepare to move out." The second blast meant to "fall into line and prepare to march." The third blast (the last trump) meant to "march away". Thus it is clear that what Paul meant was that when the last trump of this age of Grace is sounded we shall be called away to forever be with our Lord.

What a blessed hope we as believers have. *"Beloved, now are we the sons of God, and it doth not yet appear what we shall be: but we know that, when he shall appear, we shall be like him; for we shall see him as he is."* (I John 3:2). It is no wonder that Paul said: *"Wherefore comfort one another with these words."* (I Thessalonians 4:18).

CHAPTER NINE

THE BLESSED HOPE

It is important, as we draw this study to a close, to again remind you that the Bible makes a clear distinction between Israel and the Church. That is the essence of Paul's thought in Hebrews 10:9 where he states: *"Then said he, Lo, I come to do thy will, O God. He taketh away the first, that he may establish the second."* For Israel, it was atonement (a covering). For the Church, it is reconciliation through the shed blood of Christ. For Israel, the covering was a temporary dealing with their sins as they waited and looked forward to the final sacrifice (that of Yeshua at Calvary) which would eternally remove their sin. Israel looked forward to the eternal Divine Sacrifice. We have the privilege to look back to its completion. Understanding this distinction is absolutely essential to rightly dividing the Word of truth.

The Purpose for the Rapture

It is also necessary for us to understand that there is a clear distinction in Scripture between the believing Church and the institutional Church which includes both believers and non-believers. As one studies the issue of the Rapture he must keep these distinctions clearly in mind. The unbelieving apostate Church will go into the Tribulation and, along with the rest of the world, it will be judged. But this is not so for the true believing Church. The purpose of the Rapture is to finish the salvation of the true believers and present them to the Father as Christ's holy bride. As the believer is sanctified (set apart) for Christ the moment he is saved there is no longer any need for judgment of sin. The believer's sins were judged at Calvary. Through Christ's sacrifice at Calvary *"we are sanctified through the offering of the body of Jesus Christ once for all."* (Heb. 10:10).

The Character of God and the Value of the Atonement for the Church

The word "atonement" is used only once in the New Testament. In the Old Testament it literally means "to cover". The Greek word used by Paul in Rom. 5:11 is *katallasso* and is the same word he used in verse 10 that is translated "reconciled". Harper's Bible Dictionary states: "The various N.T. writings relate atonement to the suffering and sacrificial death of the sinless Jesus Christ on the Cross. By this act man is emancipated from judgment and the consequences of sin, and new life (regeneration) is made possible."[xiii] If, through the Atonement, the believer is emancipated from the judgment of sins God would be unjust to cause the believing Church to go into or through any portion of the Tribulation. Speaking of the value of the atonement (reconciliation) purchased on our behalf by Christ Paul states: *"Much more then, being justified by His blood, we shall be saved from wrath through him."* (Rom. 5:9; cf. Rom. 5:8-11).

One of the most overwhelming arguments against the believing Church going into and through any part of the Tribulation, notwithstanding God's promise to save it from the wrath to come, is the fact that the true believing Church is the Bride of Christ and Christ is the head of the true Church. Paul stated: *"But we all, with open face beholding as in a glass the glory of the Lord, are changed into the same image from glory to glory, even as by the Spirit of the Lord."* (II Cor. 3:18). This verse speaks of the believer's positional sanctification at the moment of salvation and also of a process whereby the believer is being changed into our Lord's image (practical sanctification) from glory to glory. The doctrine of sanctification precludes the Church experiencing God's wrath which is to be poured out on the unbelieving world. We are positionally sanctified in Him the moment we believe (Heb. 10:10). We spend the rest of our life, from the time we are saved to the time we go home to be with Him, being sanctified in the practical sense, a process that is completed the moment we enter into His presence (I Jn. 3:2). If we are Christ's Bride and He is our Head and He has, by His shed blood, positionally sanctified us, putting the true believing Church through any portion of the outpouring of God's wrath upon the unbelieving world would negate His promise to the Church that His blood has cleansed us from all sin, and would thus make God a liar. It would negate the sanctifying work of the Holy Spirit in the life of the believer in the Church Age. How can a sanctified Church with Christ at its head go into and through any portion of the outpouring of God's wrath? Did not Jesus take God's entire wrath upon Himself on our behalf at the cross? The character of God and the character of the true Church is the strongest argument for the pre-tribulation Rapture of the Church.

As there will be people saved during the Tribulation, it must again be pointed out that those saved during the Tribulation are never identified as the Church. They are simply identified as Tribulation saints (Rev. 13:7, 10; 14:12; 16:6; 17:6; 18:24) and are martyred. Those who survive the Tribulation long enough to see Christ return will, at that time, recognize Him for who He is, repent of their sin, receive Him as Redeemer and enter into the Millennial Kingdom a redeemed people. So, what applies to the Church cannot be applied to the Tribulation saints.

The Testimony of the Early Church

We have taken great pains to show that the pre-tribulation Rapture of the Church was the hope and teaching of the early Church by the apostles. They understood the importance of the Old Testament shadows given in the persons of Enoch and Elijah and the teaching of Isaiah and Zephaniah. We have shown the clear differences between the Revelation of Christ (the second coming) and the Rapture pointing up the difference in purpose.

The Testimony of the Ancient Church Fathers

It is clear, if one studies the writings of the early Church fathers, that the doctrine of the imminent and pre-tribulation return of Christ for His Church was clearly understood and taught. One may study the writings of Clement, Ignatius, Justin Martyr and others and see that this was the faith of the early Church fathers. Likewise, a study of the Reformers would produce the same result. For example, study Calvin's commentary on I Thessalonians 4:15. William Tyndale stated: "We are commanded to look every hour for that day," and "Christ and His apostles taught no other, but warned to look for His coming again every hour."[xiv]

The Importance of Daniel 9:20-27

We have noted the importance of understanding to whom the prophecy of the 70 weeks of years applies and how the 70th week, which is awaiting fulfillment, is the seven-year Tribulation that relates to Israel and not the Church. Many scholars place the Church Age in the parenthesis between the 69th and 70th weeks. Verse 26 necessitates a parenthesis between the cutting off of Messiah and the coming of the Prince who, according to verse 27, confirms the covenant that precipitates the beginning of the seventieth week. History proves that the Church was established after the cutting off of Messiah thus placing it squarely in the parenthesis. As the Church is not mentioned in any other passage of Scripture relating to the fulfillment of Daniel's 70th week, and as this prophecy relates most specifically to Israel and Daniel's people, there is no scriptural support for the Church to go into or through any part of that final week.

Time for Church Events Before the Revelation

There are at least two major events that occur, according to Scripture, between the Rapture and the Second Coming. Any understanding of the timing of the Rapture must include time for the Church to appear before the Judgment Seat of Christ and for the marriage ceremony to take place before the Second Coming. Only a pre-tribulation Rapture allows for the necessary time for these events.

Typology and the Rapture

We have shown that typology supports a pre-tribulation Rapture view. The principle established by God in dealing with Lot and his family in relation to the impending judgment upon Sodom and Gomorrah shows the necessity for the removal of the true Church before the judgments of the Tribulation could begin. Both Isaiah 26:19-21 and Zephaniah 2:1-3 re-affirm God's heart to remove those who are His own before great judgment could fall on the unbelieving world. The typology established by Jesus Himself as recorded in John 14:1-3 regarding the Jewish marriage customs gives us strong New Testament support of the typology established in the Old Testament. Dr. Logsdon stated: "With Noah it was "Come in" (Gen.

7:1); with Lot it was "Come out" (Gen. 19:22); and with the Church it will be "Come up" (I Thess. 4:16, 17). In each instance God delivers His own from the judgment which He Himself imposes while unbelievers must experience what they are now laying up for themselves."[xv]

The Revelation of Anti-Christ

We have learned that the anti-Christ cannot be revealed until the restrainer is removed. Restraining sin is one of the responsibilities of the Holy Spirit during the Church Age. True believers (the true Church) are indwelt by the Holy Spirit the moment they believe and continue to be indwelt as long as they are here on the earth. That is God's unconditional promise. Therefore, the true Church must be removed before anti-Christ can be revealed. The revelation of anti-Christ is the event that triggers the Tribulation. Thus the Church must be removed before the Tribulation can begin.

The Importance of the Imminent Return

If our Lord's return is imminent, there are no signs or indicators that must precede His appearing. If the Church were to go through any part of the Tribulation they would know the time. The Tribulation itself would be a necessary sign. But, God's word teaches that the timing of the Rapture is secret, surprising, and sudden without any signs.

The purpose of God for the imminent return is to motivate true believers to prepare themselves to be ready for His coming at any time. This fits the context Jesus used in John 14 of the wedding customs of His day. From the time that the groom leaves after the betrothal until He returns for His bride, is the time that the bride is to busy herself in preparations for the groom's return. In the light of those customs the bride was assured of his return. But she did not know when he would come. Only the pre-tribulation Rapture fits the type. And only the imminent return (His possible coming at any moment) gives strong motivation for believers to get ready for His appearing. The greatest joy of the true believer will be when he (she) sees the Saviour and hears Him say: "Well done, thou good and faithful servant." Apart from His already bestowed unconditional love there is no stronger motivation for godly living. This is, indeed, a Blessed Hope!

As we began this study so let us conclude it. *"And every man that hath this hope in him purifieth himself, even as he is pure."* (I John 3:3). Even so, Lord Jesus, Come quickly.

The Study Guide

Purpose Statement:

1. What is the author's view of Scripture?
2. How does this determine how one studies the Scriptures?
3. Why is II Peter 1:19, 20 so important in establishing a foundation for understanding Scripture?

Introduction:

1. How is the "Blessed Hope" defined?
2. The purpose of the Christian walk is to allow the Holy Spirit to change us. How does the Holy Spirit work to accomplish this change?
3. Why is a clear understanding of the "Blessed Hope" important to the Christian walk?
4. Why is it important to establish God's mind on Biblical matters? (two reasons)
5. How may we accomplish this?
6. What is God's plan for Israel and how does that differ from His plan for the Church?
7. Why is it important in understanding Scripture to understand God's unique plan for Israel as Opposed to His unique plan for the Church?

Chapter One:

1. What is the Second Coming?
2. What is the fourfold purpose of the Second coming?
3. How does the Second coming of our Lord affect Jew and Gentile?
4. For what Divine purpose is the Second Coming?

Chapter Two:

1. The term "rapture" is not a biblical term. Is there a biblical term that has the same meaning?

2. How would you define the term "Rapture" as used in a biblical sense?

3. How does the Rapture differ from the Second Coming? Can they be the same event?

4. What is the specific purpose of the Rapture and for whom?

Chapter 3:

1. Daniel's prophecy found in Daniel 9:20-27, according to verse 24 is about what two things?

2. Historically, what was the beginning point of this prophecy and how can we be sure?

3. What is God's six-fold purpose for these 70 weeks of years and for whom?

4. What evidence do we have that there is a parenthesis between the 69th and 70th week?

5. What is God's purpose for this parenthesis and why?

6. What evidence do we have to indicate that Daniel's 70th week is what we know as the week of Tribulation?

7. According to Daniel's prophecy, what role does the Church play in the final week of years?

8. At this point, why is it important that we make a distinction between the true believing Church And the false institutional church?

9. Why is Daniel's prophecy important to the discussion of the Blessed Hope?

Chapter 4:

1. What role does the Old Testament play in helping us to understand the message of the New Testament?

2. Why is it important for us to establish how God deals with the righteous when He is about to bring judgment upon the unrighteous?

3. How does God's dealings with Noah, Abraham and Lot, and Israel in their wilderness wanderings Help us to determine if a pattern is established?

4. What is the significance of Isaiah 26:19-21 and Zephaniah 2:1-3?

5. In the light of these references what pattern, if any, is established and how does this help us Understand the real message of the "Blessed Hope"?

Chapter 5:

1. What is God's stated purpose for the Tribulation?

2. What is the importance of the doctrine of justification as it relates to the true Church and the Tribulation?

3. Why must the Rapture occur before the beginning of the Tribulation?

4. Are the Tribulation saints a part of the Church? What evidence do we have to support your Answer? (two reasons).

5. What two events, according to Scripture, must occur between the Rapture and the Second Coming?

6. How do these events enable us to determine the timing of the Rapture?

Chapter 6:

1. How does the timing of the revelation of the anti-Christ contribute to an understanding of the timing of the rapture?

2. What must be removed from the scene before anti-Christ can be revealed?

3. Why is it necessary for the true Church to be removed before anti-Christ can be revealed?

Chapter 7:

1. What is the evidence to support the idea of the imminent return of Christ?

2. What three conclusions may we draw from the study of this chapter?

3. How does this affect our view of the timing of the Rapture?

Chapter 8:

1. How do some interpret the phrase "The last trump" so that it provides an argument against the pre-tribulation Rapture?

2. What are the three problems confronting this view?

3. What is the historical meaning of the phrase "The lost trump?

4. How does this relate to the issue of the pre-tribulation rapture?

Chapter 9:

1. What is the difference between Atonement (Kafar) in the Old Testament and Reconciliation In the New Testament?

2. What is God's purpose for the true believing Church in the Rapture?

3. How does our view of the timing of the Rapture affect our understanding of the Character of God?

4. Apart from the issue of Christ's work completed at Calvary what are the seven other reasons Given by the author as to why the Rapture must occur before the tribulation necessitating a pre- tribulation Rapture?

5. What is God's purpose in the concept of the imminent return of our Lord?

END NOTES

i   Scofield, C.I.. *Rightly Dividing The Word Of Truth*, Zondervan Publishing House, Grand Rapids, 1973; p 13

ii   Pentecost, J. D. *Things To Come*, Dunham Publishing Co., Grand Rapids, 1958; pp 201-02

iii   Webster, Noah, *Webster's New Twentieth Century Dictionary*, the World Publishing Co. New York, 1968; p.1939

iv   Anderson, Sir Robert, *The Coming Prince*; Grand Rapids:Kregel Publications, 1954, pp. 122-128

v   Logsdon, S. Franklin. *The Church Will Not Go Through The Tribulation*, Regular Baptist Press, Schaumberg, IL 1980; p. 4

vi   Steveson, Peter. *A Commentary on Isaiah*, BJU Press, Greenville, SC, 2003; p. xxiv

vii   Ibid; p. 215

viii Henry, *Matthew, Commentary on the Whole Bible, Zondervan Publishing House*, Grand Rapids, 1961; p. 1168

ix   Green, Oliver B. *Revelation, Verse By Verse*, The Gospel Hour, Greenville, SC, 1963; p 470

x   Shelton, Bob. *God's Prophetic Blueprint*, BJU Press, Greenville, SC, 1929; pp 7-8

xi   Showers, Renald. *Maranatha Our Lord, Come!* FOI, Bellmawr, NJ 1995; p 149

xii   Ibid, p 149

xiii Miller & Miller. *Harper's Bible Dictionary*, Harper & Bros. NY. p. 52

xiv Silver, Jesse F. *"The Lord's Return"*; 5th edition, Fleming H. Revell Co. NY. p. 122

xv   Logsdon, S. Franklin; ibid p. 11